Introduction

As you hold this book in your hands, you are embarking on a journey that has the potential to change your financial future. Options trading can seem daunting and complex, but it doesn't have to be. With the guidance and insights provided in "The Perfect Trade | Options Made Simple: A Beginner's Guide to Profitable Options Trading," you can learn how to trade options with confidence and success.

This book is written for anyone who wants to learn about options trading, regardless of their previous knowledge or experience. Whether you are a complete beginner or have dabbled in options trading before, this book will give you the tools and strategies you need to make informed decisions and achieve your financial goals.

At its core, options trading is about making educated predictions about the future direction of the stock market.

By buying and selling options contracts, you can profit from market movements without having to invest large sums of money. But options trading is not a get-rich-quick scheme. It's going to take time, discipline and willingness to learn.

In "The Perfect Trade," you will learn about the different types of options contracts, how to read and interpret options charts, and how to develop a trading plan that suits your individual needs and goals. You will also learn about the risks and rewards of options trading, and how to manage your trades to minimize losses and maximize profits.

But this book is not just about theory and strategy. It is also about the mindset and habits that are essential for success in options trading. You will learn how to cultivate a patient, disciplined approach to trading, how to manage your emotions and avoid impulsive decisions, and how to stay focused on your long-term goals.

Ultimately, the goal of "The Perfect Trade" is to empower you to take control of your financial future. By understanding the principles and practices of options trading, you can make informed decisions that will help you achieve your goals and build a more secure financial future for yourself and your loved ones.

So, whether you are looking to supplement your income, save for retirement, or achieve financial freedom, "The Perfect Trade | Options Made Simple: A Beginner's Guide to Profitable Options Trading" is the perfect starting point. With its clear, practical advice and actionable

The Perfect Trade

Options Made Simple: *A Beginner's Guide to Profitable Options Trading*

By Anurag Patel

Committed to all the challenges and obstacles I encountered in life. We seldom desire them, but upon contemplation, I recognise they are the foundation of my present journey.

CONTENTS

recommendations, this book will give you the tools and confidence you need to succeed in the exciting world of options trading.

CHAPTER 1

Understanding Options Basics

O ptions trading can be a complex concept to grasp, but understanding the basics is essential for anyone interested in exploring the financial market. In simple terms, options are financial derivatives that give traders the right, but not the obligation, to buy or sell an underlying asset at a predetermined price within a specific timeframe.

How Do they work?

Options provide traders with opportunities to profit from price fluctuations while offering flexibility and limited risk. There are two types of options: calls and puts. A call option gives the holder the right to buy an asset at a specified price, while a put option gives the holder the right to buy an asset at a specified price, while a put option gives them the right to sell it. Traders can enter into these options contracts by paying a premium.

The underlying asset could be stocks, commodities, currencies, or even indices. Options work by leveraging these assets' potential movements and allowing traders to speculate on future prices without owning them outright.

One of the main advantages of options trading is its versatility and ability to provide strategic hedging against market risks. Traders can use various strategies like buying or selling options or combining different positions to maximise returns or protect existing investments.

However, it is important to note that options trading also involves risks. If traders do not correctly predict market movements or exercise caution with their strategies, they may face potential losses including the entire premium paid for entering into an option contract.

Overall, understanding how options work is crucial when venturing into this market. It opens up possibilities for diversification and potentially lucrative opportunities when approached with knowledge and careful consideration. Whether as part of a comprehensive investment strategy or for short-term speculation purposes, mastering options trading can provide individuals with a powerful tool for capitalising on market movements while managing risk effectively.

Call and Put Options

For those interested in expanding their knowledge of the financial markets, understanding options trading is essential. Two fundamental components of options trading are call and put options. These terms refer to the rights, but not obligations, to buy or sell an underlying asset at a predetermined price within a specified timeframe.

A call option grants the holder the right to buy an asset, such as stocks or commodities, at a predetermined price known as the strike price. Investors typically use call options when they anticipate a rise in the price of the underlying asset.

On the other hand, a put option gives the holder the right to sell an asset at its strike price. Put options are commonly utilised by investors who expect a decline in the value of the underlying asset.

Options provide traders with flexibility and enable them to profit from both rising and falling markets. By leveraging call-and-put options effectively, investors can navigate shifts in market conditions more strategically and potentially enhance their investment returns.

Whether you are new to investing or seeking to diversify your portfolio, understanding how call and put options function is crucial for navigating more nuanced trading strategies successfully.

price, while a put option gives the holder the right to buy an asset at a specified price, while a put option gives them the right to sell it. Traders can enter into these options contracts by paying a premium.

The underlying asset could be stocks, commodities, currencies, or even indices. Options work by leveraging these assets' potential movements and allowing traders to speculate on future prices without owning them outright.

One of the main advantages of options trading is its versatility and ability to provide strategic hedging against market risks. Traders can use various strategies like buying or selling options or combining different positions to maximise returns or protect existing investments.

However, it is important to note that options trading also involves risks. If traders do not correctly predict market movements or exercise caution with their strategies, they may face potential losses including the entire premium paid for entering into an option contract.

Overall, understanding how options work is crucial when venturing into this market. It opens up possibilities for diversification and potentially lucrative opportunities when approached with knowledge and careful consideration. Whether as part of a comprehensive investment strategy or for short-term speculation purposes, mastering options trading can provide individuals with a powerful tool for capitalising on market movements while managing risk effectively.

Call and Put Options

For those interested in expanding their knowledge of the financial markets, understanding options trading is essential. Two fundamental components of options trading are call and put options. These terms refer to the rights, but not obligations, to buy or sell an underlying asset at a predetermined price within a specified timeframe.

A call option grants the holder the right to buy an asset, such as stocks or commodities, at a predetermined price known as the strike price. Investors typically use call options when they anticipate a rise in the price of the underlying asset.

On the other hand, a put option gives the holder the right to sell an asset at its strike price. Put options are commonly utilised by investors who expect a decline in the value of the underlying asset.

Options provide traders with flexibility and enable them to profit from both rising and falling markets. By leveraging call-and-put options effectively, investors can navigate shifts in market conditions more strategically and potentially enhance their investment returns.

Whether you are new to investing or seeking to diversify your portfolio, understanding how call and put options function is crucial for navigating more nuanced trading strategies successfully.

Option Pricing and Premium

Understanding option pricing and premium is crucial for successful options trading. Option pricing is influenced by several factors including the current price of the underlying asset, the strike price (the predetermined price), time to expiration, market volatility, and interest rates. These factors collectively contribute to the overall value of an option's premium.

When analysing options pricing, it is important to consider both intrinsic value and extrinsic value. Intrinsic value represents any profit that could be gained if the option were exercised immediately, while extrinsic value reflects factors such as time decay and implied volatility.

Traders utilise various mathematical models like Black-Scholes or binomial models to calculate option premiums based on these factors. By evaluating these premiums, traders can assess potential risks and rewards associated with different options strategies.

It is crucial for options traders to understand how the premium is priced in order to make informed decisions. Moreover, keeping track of market trends and staying updated on relevant news can help identify favourable trading opportunities with potentially higher premiums.

In conclusion, comprehending how option pricing works and analysing premiums enables traders to evaluate potential profits and risks associated with options trading strategies more effectively.

Options Expiration and Exercise

These two terms are essential to understand when trading options, as they can have a significant impact on your trading strategy.

Options expiration refers to the date on which an option contract expires. When you buy an option contract, you are essentially buying the right to buy or sell an underlying asset at a specific price (the strike price) on or before the expiration date. If the option contract expires without being exercised, it becomes worthless, and you lose the premium you paid to buy the option.

It's important to keep in mind that options have a finite lifespan, unlike stocks, which can be held indefinitely. This means that you need to be aware of the expiration date of your option contracts and take action before they expire.

Option exercise, on the other hand, refers to the act of using your option contract to buy or sell the underlying asset at the strike price. If you have a call option, you would exercise it if you wanted to buy the underlying asset at the strike price. If you have a put option, you would exercise it if you wanted to sell the underlying asset at the strike price.

When you exercise an option, you are essentially using the right that you bought when you purchased the option contract. It's important to note that there are two types of options - American and European - that have different rules regarding when they can be exercised.

American options can be exercised at any time before the expiration date, while European options can only be exercised on the expiration date itself. This means that American options are generally more valuable than European options, as they offer greater flexibility to the option holder.

Now that you understand the basics of options expiration and exercise, let's take a closer look at how they can impact your trading strategy.

First, it's important to keep in mind that options contracts can be bought and sold on the open market, just like stocks. This means that you can sell your option contract before it expires, even if you haven't exercised it.

If you have a profitable option contract that is approaching its expiration date, you may choose to sell it rather than exercise it. This allows you to lock in your profits without having to worry about the complexities of exercising the option.

However, if you have a losing option contract that is approaching its expiration date, you may choose to exercise it in an attempt to salvage some of your investment. This can be a risky strategy, as it requires you to buy or sell the underlying asset at the strike price, which may not be the most favourable price at the time of expiration.

In general, it's important to have a clear understanding of your trading strategy before you enter into any options contracts. This includes knowing when your option contracts expire, what your exit strategy is, and how you plan to manage any losses.

In conclusion, options expiration and exercise are essential concepts for option traders to understand. By knowing when your option contracts expire and how to exercise them, you can make informed decisions that support your trading strategy. Remember to always be vigilant and have a clear plan in place before entering into any options contracts.

CHAPTER 2

Risk Management in Options Trading

A s a trader, managing risk is one of the most crucial aspects of your job. Options trading can be lucrative, but it can also be incredibly risky if you don't properly manage your trades.

One of the first things you should do when managing risk in options trading is to determine your risk tolerance. This means understanding how much money you're willing to risk on a trade and what your overall goals are. Once you've determined this, you can begin to develop a trading plan that aligns with your risk tolerance and goals.

Another important factor in risk management is diversification. It's never a good idea to put all of your eggs in one basket, so to speak. Instead, spread your trades across different stocks, sectors, and strategies. This way, if one trade goes south, you won't lose everything.

You should also be aware of the different types of risks involved in options trading. The two main types of risk are market risk and specific risk. Market risk refers to the overall volatility of the market and affects all stocks, while the specific risk is unique to a particular stock or company. By diversifying your trades, you can reduce your specific risk.

In addition to diversification, it's important to set stop-loss orders. A stop-loss order is an order placed with a broker to sell a stock when it reaches a certain price. This helps to protect you from significant losses by automatically selling a stock if it drops below a certain price point.

Another important aspect of risk management is knowing when to cut your losses. If a trade isn't going as planned, it's better to cut your losses early rather than holding on and hoping for a turnaround that may never come.

Finally, keep an eye on your emotions. It's easy to get caught up in the excitement of trading, but this can lead to impulsive decisions and trades that don't align with your trading plan. Try to remain calm and rational, and always stick to your plan.

In conclusion, options trading can be a lucrative way to invest, but it's important to properly manage your risk. Determine your risk tolerance, diversify your trades, set stop-loss orders, know when to cut your losses, and keep your emotions in check. By following these guidelines, you can reduce your risk and increase your chances of success in options trading.

The Role of Risk in Trading

You are constantly looking for ways to maximise your profits while minimising your risks. However, risk is an inherent part of trading and cannot be completely eliminated. In fact, understanding and managing risk is crucial to becoming a successful trader.

One of the key concepts in trading is the risk-return tradeoff. This means that the greater the potential return on an investment, the greater the risk involved. As an option trader, you have the ability to leverage your trades and potentially earn high returns, but this also comes with a higher level of risk.

One way to manage risk is through diversification. This means spreading your investments across different assets and markets, rather than putting all your eggs in one basket. By diversifying your portfolio, you can reduce your exposure to any single asset or market and potentially minimise your losses.

Another important factor in managing risk is having a solid trading plan. This includes setting clear goals and objectives, identifying your risk tolerance, and determining your exit strategies. For example, if a trade starts to go against you, you should have a predetermined plan for cutting your losses and exiting the trade.

It's also important to stay up to date on market news and trends. This can help you make informed decisions and adjust your trading strategies accordingly. However, it's important to not let emotions cloud your judgment. Fear and greed can often lead to impulsive decisions that can result in significant losses.

One tool that option traders often use to manage risk is options spreads. This involves buying and selling options at different strike prices and expiration dates in order to limit potential losses and maximise potential profits. Options spreads can be complex, but they can also be a powerful tool in managing risk.

Finally, it's important to remember that no trading strategy can completely eliminate risk. Even the most experienced traders experience losses from time to time. The key is to manage risk in a way that allows you to stay in the game and continue trading over the long term.

In conclusion, risk is an inherent part of trading, but it can be managed through diversification, a solid trading plan, staying up to date on market news and trends, using options spreads, and managing emotions. By understanding and managing risk, option traders can potentially earn high returns while minimising their losses.

Position Sizing and Capital Allocation

One of the most important aspects of your trading strategy is position sizing and capital allocation. These are the tools you use to manage risk and maximise profits, and they can make all the difference between success and failure.

Position sizing refers to the amount of capital you allocate to each trade. This is a critical factor in managing risk, as it determines how much you stand to lose if a trade goes against you. You should never risk more than you can afford to lose, and your position size should reflect your risk tolerance and overall trading strategy.

One common approach to position sizing is to use a fixed percentage of your account balance for each trade. For example, you might decide to risk no more than 2% of your account on any given trade. This helps ensure that you don't put too much of your capital at risk on any one trade, which can help protect you from catastrophic losses.

Another approach is to use a formula based on your trading strategy and risk tolerance. For example, you might use a formula that takes into account the volatility of the underlying asset, the size of your stop loss, and your overall risk tolerance. This can be a more sophisticated approach, but it can also help you optimise your position sizing based on the specific conditions of each trade.

Capital allocation refers to the overall amount of capital you allocate to your trading account. This is another critical factor in managing risk, as it determines how much capital you have available to trade with. You should never risk more than you can afford to lose, and your overall capital allocation should reflect your risk tolerance and overall trading strategy.

One common approach to capital allocation is to use a fixed amount of capital for your trading account. For example, you might decide to allocate $10,000 to your trading account. This helps ensure that you don't put too much of your capital at risk, and it can also help you manage your emotions and avoid overtrading.

Another approach is to use a formula based on your trading strategy and risk tolerance. For example, you might use a formula that takes into account the number of trades you expect to make each month, the average size of your trades, and your overall risk tolerance. This can be a more sophisticated approach, but it can also help you optimise your capital allocation based on your trading strategy.

Ultimately, the key to successful position sizing and capital allocation is to find an approach that works for you. This might involve a combination of fixed percentages, formulas, and other factors that take into account your specific trading strategy, risk tolerance, and overall goals.

One important thing to keep in mind is that position sizing and capital allocation are not static. They should be reviewed and adjusted regularly based on your trading performance and overall market conditions. This can help you stay on track and avoid making costly mistakes.

In conclusion, position sizing and capital allocation are critical factors in managing risk and maximising profits. By finding an approach that works for you and regularly reviewing and adjusting your strategy, you can help ensure long-term success in the markets.

Stop Loss Strategies

You know that the market can be unpredictable, and losses are an inevitable part of the game. However, one way to minimise the impact of losses is by implementing stop-loss strategies.

Stop loss is a tool that helps traders limit their losses by automatically closing their positions when the price of an asset reaches a certain level. This level is predetermined by the trader, and it is usually based on the amount of risk they are willing to take.

There are different types of stop-loss strategies that traders can use, and each one has its advantages and disadvantages. In this topic, we will discuss some of the most popular ones.

1. Fixed Stop Loss

A fixed stop loss is the most common type of stop loss strategy. It is a predetermined price level that a trader sets to exit a trade if the price of an asset reaches it. This stop loss level is usually based on the trader's risk tolerance and can be adjusted according to the market conditions.

The advantage of using a fixed stop loss is that it is easy to implement and can be automated. However, the disadvantage is that it may not be effective in volatile markets, as the price may quickly reach the stop-loss level and trigger the trade exit.

2. Trailing Stop Loss

A trailing stop loss is a dynamic stop loss strategy that adjusts the stop loss level based on the price movement of the asset. It is designed to protect profits by allowing traders to lock in gains while also giving them room to ride the trend.

The way a trailing stop loss works is that it sets a percentage or a dollar value away from the current price. If the price of the asset moves in the trader's favour, the stop loss level moves with it. However, if the price of the asset moves against the trader, the stop loss level remains fixed.

The advantage of using a trailing stop loss is that it can protect profits while also giving traders room to ride the trend. However, the disadvantage is that it may not be effective in choppy markets, as the price may move back and forth, triggering the stop loss level.

3. Time Stop Loss

A time stop-loss is a strategy that involves closing a trade after a certain period, regardless of the price movement. This strategy is usually used in markets that are known for their volatility, such as the forex market.

The advantage of using a time stop-loss is that it can help traders avoid losses during periods of extreme volatility. However, the disadvantage is that it may not be effective in trending markets, as the price may continue to move in the trader's favour after the time stop-loss is triggered.

In conclusion, stop-loss strategies are an essential tool for traders who want to minimise their losses and protect their profits. Each strategy has its advantages and disadvantages, and it is up to the trader to choose the one that suits their trading style and risk tolerance. By implementing a stop-loss strategy, traders can take control of their risk and increase their chances of success in the market.

Risk-Reward Ratio

You are probably familiar with the concept of the risk-reward ratio. It is a critical metric that helps you determine whether a trade is worth taking or not. In this topic, we will explore the risk-reward ratio in more detail and explain how you can use it to make better trading decisions.

The risk-reward ratio is simply the ratio of the potential profit of a trade to its potential loss. For example, if you are considering a trade with a potential profit of $100 and a potential loss of $50, your risk-reward ratio would be 2:1. In other words, you stand to gain $2 for every $1 you risk.

Why is the risk-reward ratio important? Because it tells you whether a trade is worth taking. A high risk-reward ratio means that the potential reward is much greater than the potential risk. A low risk-reward ratio means that the potential reward is not worth the potential risk.

So how do you determine the risk-reward ratio of a trade? First, you need to know your potential profit and potential loss. This will depend on the specifics of the trade, such as the strike price, expiration date, and premium.

Once you know your potential profit and potential loss, you can calculate the risk-reward ratio. Simply divide the potential profit by the potential loss. If the ratio is high, the trade is worth considering. If the ratio is low, the trade is probably not worth taking.

Of course, the risk-reward ratio is not the only factor to consider when making trading decisions. You also need to consider your overall trading strategy, your risk tolerance, and the market conditions. But the risk-reward ratio is a crucial metric that should always be factored into your decision-making process.

So how can you use the risk-reward ratio in your trading? Here are a few tips:

1. Set a minimum risk-reward ratio. Before you enter a trade, decide on a minimum risk-reward ratio that you are willing to accept. This will help you avoid trades with low potential rewards and high potential risks.

2. Adjust your position size based on the risk-reward ratio. If a trade has a high risk-reward ratio, you may want to increase your position size to take advantage of the

potential reward. If a trade has a low risk-reward ratio, you may want to decrease your position size to limit your potential losses.

3. Use stop-loss orders to manage risk. A stop-loss order is an order to sell a security if it reaches a certain price. By using stop-loss orders, you can limit your potential losses and ensure that your trades stay within your risk-reward parameters.

In conclusion, the risk-reward ratio is a critical metric that every option trader should understand. By using the risk-reward ratio to evaluate potential trades, you can make better trading decisions and improve your overall profitability. Remember to always consider the risk-reward ratio in conjunction with your overall trading strategy and risk tolerance. With a little practice, you can become a more confident and successful option trader.

CHAPTER 3

Advanced Options Strategies

There are many strategies you can use to maximise your profits and minimise your risks. Advanced options strategies are some of the most effective tools at your disposal, but they can also be some of the most complex and difficult to understand. In this chapter, we'll explore some of the most popular advanced options strategies and discuss how they work.

One of the most popular advanced options strategies is the iron condor. This strategy involves selling both a call option and a put option at the same strike price, while buying a call option and a put option at a higher and lower strike price, respectively. The goal of this strategy is to profit from the premiums received from selling the options, while also limiting your risk by buying options at strike prices that are further away from the current market price. This strategy is best used in a market that is trading sideways, as it allows you to profit from the premiums received while minimising your risk.

Another popular advanced options strategy is the butterfly. This strategy involves buying a call option and a put option at the same strike price, while also selling two call options and two put options at higher and lower strike prices, respectively. The goal of this strategy is to profit from the price movements of the underlying asset, while also limiting your risk by buying options at the same strike price. This strategy is best used in a market that is trading within a certain range, as it allows you to profit from price movements while minimising your risk.

A third advanced options strategy is the calendar spread. This strategy involves buying a call option and a put option at the same strike price, but with different expiration dates. The goal of this strategy is to profit from the time decay of the options, while also limiting your risk by buying options at the same strike price. This strategy is best used in a market that is trading sideways, as it allows you to profit from the time decay of the options while minimising your risk.

While these are just a few of the many advanced options strategies available, they are some of the most effective and commonly used. When using advanced options strategies, it's important to keep in mind that they are more complex and difficult to understand than basic options strategies and require a high level of knowledge and experience to use effectively. It's also important to always do your research and thoroughly understand the risks and potential rewards associated with any strategy before implementing it.

In conclusion, advanced options strategies can be powerful tools for option traders looking to maximise their profits and minimise their risks. By using strategies such as the iron condor, butterfly, and calendar spread, traders can profit from premiums received, price movements, and time decay, while also limiting their risk. However, it's important to always do your research and have a solid understanding of the risks and potential rewards associated with any strategy before implementing it.

Covered Calls and Protective Puts

You're likely looking for ways to invest your money and grow your wealth. One strategy that you may want to consider is using covered calls and protective puts.

Covered calls involve selling call options on a stock that you already own. Essentially, you're giving someone else the right to buy your stock at a certain price (the strike price) by a certain date (the expiration date). In exchange for this right, the buyer of the call option pays you a premium.

If the stock price stays below the strike price, the call option will expire worthless and you get to keep the premium. If the stock price rises above the strike price, the buyer of the call option will likely exercise their right to buy your stock from you at the strike price. You'll still make a profit on the stock (since you bought it at a lower price), but you'll miss out on any potential gains above the strike price.

Protective puts involve buying put options on a stock that you already own. Put options give you the right to sell your stock at a certain price (the strike price) by a certain date (the expiration date). In exchange for this right, you pay a premium.

If the stock price drops below the strike price, the put option will increase in value and you can sell it for a profit. This profit will help offset any losses you may experience on the stock. If the stock price stays above the strike price, the put option will expire worthless and you'll lose the premium you paid.

Both covered calls and protective puts can be used to manage risk in your portfolio. Covered calls can help you generate income and limit your potential losses if the stock price rises. Protective puts can help you protect your gains and limit your potential losses if the stock price drops.

However, it's important to note that both strategies have some drawbacks. Covered calls limit your upside potential if the stock price rises above the strike price. Protective puts can be expensive and may limit your potential profits if the stock price stays above the strike price.

Before using either strategy, it's important to do your research and understand the risks involved. You should also consult with a financial advisor to determine if covered calls and/or protective puts are appropriate for your investment goals and risk tolerance.

In conclusion, covered calls and protective puts are two strategies that students may want to consider when looking to invest in the stock market. Both can be used to manage risk and potentially generate income, but they also come with some drawbacks. As with any investment strategy, it's important to do your due diligence and seek professional advice before making any decisions.

Credit and Debit Spreads

This strategy involves simultaneous buying and selling of options contracts, but they differ in some key ways. Here's what you need to know about credit and debit spreads.

Credit Spreads

A credit spread is a strategy where you sell an option contract and buy another option contract at a different strike price. The two contracts will have different expiration dates as well. The option you sell will be at a higher strike price than the option you buy. You receive a credit for selling the option, which is why it's called a credit spread.

The goal of a credit spread is to make a profit from the difference between the premiums received from selling the option and the premium paid to buy the option. If the price of the underlying asset remains within a certain range, the options will expire worthless and you keep the premium received from selling the option. If the price of the underlying asset moves outside of that range, you may have to buy back the sold option at a loss.

Debit Spreads

A debit spread is a strategy where you buy an option contract and sell another option contract at a different strike price. The two contracts will have different expiration dates as well. The option you buy will be at a higher strike price than the option you sell. You pay a debit for buying the option, which is why it's called a debit spread.

The goal of a debit spread is to make a profit from the difference between the premiums paid to buy the option and the premium received from selling the option. If the price of the underlying asset moves within a certain range, the options will expire worthless and you will lose the premium paid to buy the option. If the price of the underlying asset moves outside of that range, you may be able to sell the bought option at a profit.

Which One Should You Use?

The choice between a credit and debit spread depends on your market outlook. If you believe that the price of the underlying asset will remain within a certain range, a credit spread may be the better choice. If you believe that the price of the underlying asset will move outside of that range, a debit spread may be the better choice.

Credit spreads have a higher probability of success because the price of the underlying asset only needs to stay within a certain range for the options to expire worthless. Debit spreads have a lower probability of success because the price of the underlying asset needs to move outside of a certain range for the options to be profitable.

Conclusion

Credit and debit spreads are two of the most popular options trading strategies. They involve buying and selling option contracts at different strike prices and expiration dates. Credit spreads involve selling an option contract and buying another option contract at a different strike price, while debit spreads involve buying an option contract and selling another option contract at a different strike price. The choice between a credit and debit spread depends on your market outlook.

Iron Condors and Butterflies

Two popular strategies that you may have heard of are the Iron Condor and the Butterfly. While both strategies involve trading options with multiple legs, they have different risk and reward profiles. In this topic, we will explore the Iron Condor and the Butterfly and highlight their similarities and differences.

What is an Iron Condor?

An Iron Condor is a four-legged options strategy that involves selling both a call spread and a put spread with the same expiration date. The call spread is a bearish strategy that involves selling a call option at a higher strike price while buying a call option at a lower strike price. The put spread is a bullish strategy that involves selling a put option at a lower strike price while buying a put option at a higher strike price. The goal of the Iron Condor is to profit from the time decay of the options while minimising risk.

The maximum profit for an Iron Condor is the net credit received from selling the options. The maximum loss is the difference between the strike prices of the call spread minus the net credit received or the difference between the strike prices of the put spread minus the net credit received. The Iron Condor is a neutral strategy, meaning it makes money when the underlying stock stays within a certain range. If the stock moves too far in either direction, the Iron Condor will incur losses.

What is a Butterfly?

A Butterfly is a three-legged options strategy that involves buying one call option at a lower strike price, selling two call options at a middle strike price, and buying one call option at a higher strike price. The goal of the Butterfly is to profit from a small move in the underlying stock while limiting risk.

The maximum profit for a Butterfly is achieved when the underlying stock is at the middle strike price at expiration. The maximum loss is the net debit paid for the options. The Butterfly is a neutral strategy, meaning it makes money when the underlying stock stays within a certain range. If the stock moves too far in either direction, the Butterfly will incur losses.

Similarities and Differences

Both the Iron Condor and the Butterfly are neutral strategies that involve trading options with multiple legs. They both profit from the time decay of the options and have limited risk. However, there are some key differences.

The Iron Condor has four legs and involves selling both a call spread and a put spread. The Butterfly has three legs and involves buying one call option at a lower strike price, selling two call options at a middle strike price, and buying one call option at a higher strike price.

The Iron Condor has a wider range of profitability and a higher maximum profit potential than the Butterfly. However, the Iron Condor also has a higher maximum loss potential. The Butterfly has a smaller range of profitability and a lower maximum profit potential than the Iron Condor. However, the Butterfly also has a lower maximum loss potential.

Conclusion

It's important to understand the different strategies available to you and their risk and reward profiles. The Iron Condor and the Butterfly are two popular strategies that can be used to profit from a neutral market. While they have similarities, they also have differences in terms of leg count, profitability range, and maximum risk and reward potential. By understanding these differences, you can choose the strategy that best fits your trading style and risk tolerance.

Straddles and Strangles

A straddle involves buying both a call option and a put option at the same strike price and expiration date. The idea behind a straddle is that you are betting on a significant move in the underlying stock, regardless of whether it goes up or down. If the stock stays relatively stable, you will likely lose money on both options. However, if there is a large move in either direction, you stand to make a profit.

A strangle, on the other hand, involves buying both a call option and a put option, but at different strike prices. The idea behind a strangle is similar to a straddle in that you are betting on volatility, but the difference in strike prices means that the stock needs to move even further in order for you to make a profit. The risk is lower with a strangle than with a straddle, but so is the potential payoff.

When deciding whether to use a straddle or a strangle, it's important to consider your risk tolerance and your outlook for the underlying stock. A straddle is a higher-risk strategy with the potential for higher returns, but it requires a larger move in the stock price. A strangle is a lower-risk strategy with a lower potential payout, but it requires a more modest move in the stock price.

Another consideration when using these strategies is timing. Because both straddles and strangles involve buying options, they are subject to time decay. This means that the options lose value over time, even if the stock price remains the same. As a result, it's important to choose expiration dates that give the stock enough time to move, but not so much time that the options lose too much value.

In addition to timing, it's important to consider the volatility of the underlying stock. Both straddles and strangles are designed to profit from volatility, but if the stock is too volatile, it can be difficult to predict which way it will move. This can lead to losses on both the call and put options.

Finally, it's important to have a plan in place for managing risk. Because both straddles and strangles involve buying options, they are limited risk strategies. However, it's still possible to lose money if the stock doesn't move as expected. By setting stop-loss orders and monitoring your positions closely, you can limit your losses and protect your profits.

In conclusion, straddles and strangles are two popular options trading strategies that can be used to profit from volatility in the market. While both strategies involve buying call-and-put options, they differ in their risk and payoff potential. By considering your risk tolerance, outlook for the underlying stock, timing, and volatility, you can choose the right strategy for your trading needs. And by having a plan in place for managing risk, you can protect your profits and limit your losses.

CHAPTER 4

Chart Reading and Technical Analysis

T he importance of chart reading and technical analysis in making informed investment decisions. While there are many different strategies and tools available to traders, chart reading and technical analysis are two key components that many find particularly helpful.

At its most basic level, chart reading involves analysing historical price and volume data in order to identify patterns and trends that can provide insight into future market movements. Technical analysis takes this a step further, using a variety of technical indicators and statistical models to help traders identify potential buy and sell signals.

One of the most important things to keep in mind when using chart reading and technical analysis is that these tools are not foolproof. They are just one piece of the puzzle when it comes to making investment decisions, and should be used in conjunction with other sources of information and analysis.

That being said, there are several key benefits to incorporating chart reading and technical analysis into your trading strategy. One of the most obvious is that it can help you identify potential entry and exit points for trades. By analysing historical price data and looking for patterns and trends, you can get a better sense of when a particular stock or market is likely to experience a significant price movement.

Another benefit of chart reading and technical analysis is that it can help you better understand market psychology and sentiment. By analysing the behaviour of other traders and investors, you can get a better sense of how the market as a whole is feeling about a particular stock or sector. This can help you make more informed decisions about when to buy or sell.

Of course, one of the challenges of using chart reading and technical analysis is that it can be quite complex and difficult to master. There is a wide variety of technical indicators and chart patterns to learn about, and it can take a significant amount of time and effort to become proficient.

One way to make the process a bit easier is to start by focusing on just a few key indicators or patterns. Some popular options include moving averages, relative strength index (RSI), and support and resistance levels. By mastering these basics, you can begin to develop a more in-depth understanding of how technical analysis works and how it can be used in your trading strategy.

Another important consideration when using chart reading and technical analysis is to be mindful of potential biases and pitfalls. For example, it can be easy to fall into the trap of confirmation bias, where you only look for data that supports your existing beliefs about a particular stock or market. Similarly, it's important to be wary of over-reliance on any single indicator or pattern, as this can lead to false signals and poor investment decisions.

Ultimately, if you're a stock market enthusiast looking to take your trading strategy to the next level, chart reading and technical analysis can be powerful tools to have in your arsenal. While they require time and effort to master, they can help you identify potential opportunities and make more informed decisions about when to buy and sell. Just be sure to keep in mind that they are just one piece of the puzzle, and should be used in conjunction with other sources of information and analysis.

Introduction to Technical Analysis

Technical analysis is an essential tool that traders use to make sense of market movements and predict future trends. It is the process of studying historical market data, such as price and volume, to identify patterns and trends. The goal is to use this information to predict future market movements, allowing traders to make informed decisions about buying and selling assets.

One of the primary benefits of technical analysis is that it can help traders to identify key levels of support and resistance. These are price levels at which the market has historically struggled to rise above or fall below. By identifying these levels, traders can make informed decisions about when to enter and exit trades, maximising their profits and minimising their losses.

Another key aspect of technical analysis is the use of indicators. These are mathematical calculations that use historical market data to provide traders with insights into market trends and patterns. Some common indicators include moving averages, relative strength index (RSI), and Bollinger Bands.

Moving averages are used to smooth out market data over a specified period, providing traders with a clearer picture of the overall trend. The RSI is used to identify overbought and oversold conditions in the market, indicating when a reversal may be imminent. Bollinger Bands are used to identify the volatility of a market, providing traders with insights into potential price movements.

While technical analysis is a powerful tool, it is not without its limitations. One of the most significant drawbacks is that it is based entirely on historical data and does not take into account external factors that may impact the market. For example, unexpected news events or changes in government policy can have a significant impact on market movements, rendering technical analysis less effective.

Another limitation is that technical analysis can be complex and time-consuming. Traders must be willing to spend time analysing market data and interpreting indicators to make informed decisions. Additionally, it is essential to have a solid understanding of market fundamentals to ensure that technical analysis is used in conjunction with other tools and strategies to maximise profits.

In conclusion, technical analysis is a powerful tool that traders can use to make informed decisions about buying and selling assets. By analysing historical market data and using indicators to identify patterns and trends, traders can identify key levels of support and resistance and make informed decisions about when to enter and exit trades. While technical analysis is not without its limitations, it remains an essential tool for traders looking to maximise their profits and minimise their losses.

Candlestick Patterns and Their Interpretation

Candlestick patterns are a visual representation of the price movement of an asset over a specific period of time. They are made up of a series of candles, each of which represents a specific time frame, such as a day, an hour, or even a minute. Each candle has four main components: the opening price, the closing price, the high price, and the low price.

Candlestick patterns are used to identify trends and potential reversals in the market. They can be used in conjunction with other technical indicators to form a comprehensive trading strategy. In this topic, we will look at some of the most common candlestick patterns and how they can be interpreted.

1. Doji

A Doji candlestick pattern is formed when the opening and closing prices of an asset are almost the same. It indicates indecision in the market and can be a sign of a potential trend reversal. If a Doji candlestick pattern appears after a long uptrend, it could mean that the bulls are losing their momentum and the bears are gaining control.

2. Hammer

A Hammer candlestick pattern is formed when the opening and closing prices are close to each other, but the low price is significantly lower than the opening and closing prices. It looks like a hammer, hence the name. This pattern is a bullish reversal pattern and indicates that the bulls are gaining control after a period of bearishness.

3. Shooting Star

A Shooting Star candlestick pattern is the opposite of the Hammer pattern. It is formed when the high price is significantly higher than the opening and closing prices, and the low price is close to the opening and closing prices. It looks like a shooting star, hence the name. This pattern is a bearish reversal pattern and indicates that the bears are gaining control after a period of bullishness.

4. Engulfing

An Engulfing candlestick pattern is formed when a small candle is followed by a much larger candle that completely engulfs the previous candle. If the second candle is bullish, it is a bullish reversal pattern, indicating that the bulls are gaining control after a period of bearishness. If the second candle is bearish, it is a bearish reversal pattern, indicating that the bears are gaining control after a period of bullishness.

5. Morning Star

A Morning Star candlestick pattern is formed by three candles: a long bearish candle, followed by a small bullish or bearish candle, and then a long bullish candle. This pattern is a bullish reversal pattern and indicates that the bulls are gaining control after a period of bearishness.

In conclusion, candlestick patterns are a powerful tool that can help options traders to identify trends and potential reversals in the market. By understanding the various patterns and their interpretations, traders can form a comprehensive trading strategy that can help them maximise their profits and minimise their losses. However, it is important to note that candlestick patterns should not be used in isolation and should be used in conjunction with other technical indicators for maximum effectiveness.

Support and Resistance Levels

Support and resistance levels are critical components of technical analysis, which is an approach to trading that involves studying charts and identifying patterns and trends.

Support levels are price levels where demand for an asset is strong enough to prevent it from falling further. When an asset's price reaches a support level, traders often see it as a good buying opportunity, as they believe the asset will rebound from that level. Conversely, resistance levels are price levels where the supply for an asset is strong enough to prevent it from rising further. When an asset's price reaches a resistance level, traders often see it as a good selling opportunity, as they believe the asset will fall from that level.

Identifying support and resistance levels is not always a straightforward process. Traders use a variety of tools and techniques to identify these levels, including trendlines, moving averages, and Fibonacci retracements. Once identified, support and resistance levels can be used to make trading decisions, such as setting stop-loss orders or taking profits.

One of the most popular methods for identifying support and resistance levels is drawing trendlines. A trendline is a straight line that connects two or more price points on a chart. When drawing a trendline, traders are looking for areas where the price has reversed direction in the past. These areas can be interpreted as support or resistance levels, depending on whether the price is currently above or below the trendline.

Moving averages are another tool used to identify support and resistance levels. A moving average is a line that represents the average price of an asset over a specific period of time. Traders often use moving averages to identify trends in an asset's price, and to identify potential support or resistance levels. For example, if an asset's price is currently below its 50-day moving average, traders may see that level as a potential resistance level.

Fibonacci retracements are a more advanced technique for identifying support and resistance levels. Fibonacci retracements are based on the idea that markets tend to retrace a predictable portion of a move, after which they will continue to move in the original direction. Traders use Fibonacci retracements to identify potential support or resistance levels based on these predictable retracement levels.

Once support and resistance levels have been identified, traders can use them to make trading decisions. For example, if a trader identifies a strong support level for an asset, they may set a stop-loss order just below that level to protect themselves in case the asset's price falls further. Alternatively, if a trader identifies a strong resistance level for an asset, they may take profits on a long position just below that level, as they believe the asset will fall from that point.

In conclusion, understanding support and resistance levels is essential for options traders. These levels are critical components of technical analysis and can be used to make trading decisions such as setting stop-loss orders or taking profits. Traders use a variety of tools and techniques to identify support and resistance levels, including trendlines, moving averages, and Fibonacci retracements. By mastering these tools and techniques, traders can gain a deeper understanding of market trends and make more informed trading decisions.

Moving Averages and Oscillators

Moving averages are a simple yet effective tool used to identify trends in the market. The moving average is calculated by taking the average price of a security over a specified period of time. For example, a 50-day moving average would take the average price of a security over the past 50 days. Traders use moving averages to identify the direction of the trend. If the security's price is above the moving average, it is considered to be in an uptrend. Conversely, if the security's price is below the moving average, it is considered to be in a downtrend.

Oscillators are another popular tool used in technical analysis. Oscillators are indicators that move back and forth between two extremes. They are used to identify overbought and oversold conditions in the market. When an oscillator reaches an extreme level, it is considered to be overbought or oversold. Traders use this information to identify potential trading opportunities. For example, if an oscillator reaches an overbought level, it may signal that the security is due for a pullback.

One popular oscillator used by traders is the Relative Strength Index (RSI). The RSI is a momentum oscillator that measures the speed and change of price movements. The RSI ranges from 0 to 100 and is considered overbought when it is above 70 and oversold when it is below 30. Traders use the RSI to identify potential trend reversals. For example, if the RSI is in overbought territory and starts to move lower, it may signal that the security is due for a pullback.

Another popular oscillator used by traders is the Moving Average Convergence Divergence (MACD). The MACD is a trend-following momentum indicator that shows the relationship between two moving averages of a security's price. The MACD is calculated by subtracting the 26-day exponential moving average (EMA) from the 12-day EMA. A nine-day EMA of the MACD, called the "signal line", is then plotted on top of the MACD. Traders use the MACD to identify potential trend reversals. For example, if the MACD crosses above the signal line, it may signal that the security is entering an uptrend.

In conclusion, moving averages and oscillators are popular tools used by options traders to identify trends and potential trading opportunities. Moving averages are used to identify the direction of the trend, while oscillators are used to identify overbought and oversold conditions in the market. Traders use these tools in combination with other technical analysis tools to develop a comprehensive trading strategy. By using these tools, options traders can make more informed trading decisions and improve their chances of success in the market.

CHAPTER 5

Volatility Trading

You know how important it is to stay on top of market movements and trends. One strategy that can help you capitalise on market volatility is volatility trading.

Volatility trading involves taking advantage of price fluctuations in the market, specifically in the implied volatility of options. Implied volatility represents the market's expectation of how much a stock's price will fluctuate in the future. When implied volatility is high, options prices tend to be more expensive, and when implied volatility is low, options prices tend to be cheaper.

One way to trade volatility is through options straddles or strangles. These strategies involve buying both a call option and a put option at the same strike price and expiration date (straddle) or at different strike prices but the same expiration date (strangle). The idea behind these strategies is that if the stock price moves significantly in either direction, one of the options will be profitable, and the profits from that option will offset the losses from the other option.

Another way to trade volatility is through options spreads. Options spreads involve buying and selling options at different strike prices and expiration dates to create a net debit or credit. For example, a bull call spread involves buying a call option at a lower strike price and selling a call option at a higher strike price. The idea behind this strategy is that the profits from the lower strike call option will offset the losses from the higher strike call option, resulting in a net profit if the stock price increases. This strategy is useful in a low-volatility environment where options prices are cheaper.

A third way to trade volatility is through the use of exchange-traded funds (ETFs) that track volatility indexes. One such ETF is the VIX, which tracks the CBOE Volatility Index. This index measures the market's expectation of volatility over the next 30 days. When the VIX is high, it represents increased fear and uncertainty in the market, and when the VIX is low, it represents increased confidence and stability in the market. By trading VIX ETFs, traders can take advantage of market volatility without having to trade individual stocks.

As with any trading strategy, there are risks involved in volatility trading. One of the biggest risks is timing. It can be difficult to predict when volatility will increase or decrease, and if you enter a trade at the wrong time, you could suffer significant losses. Another risk is that options prices can be highly volatile, which means that the price of the options can change rapidly and unpredictably. This can result in significant losses if you are not careful.

To mitigate these risks, it is important to have a solid understanding of options trading and to have a well-defined trading plan. This plan should include entry and exit points, as well as risk management strategies such as stop-loss orders. It is also important to stay up-to-date on market news and trends, as well as to monitor the implied volatility of options to identify trading opportunities.

In conclusion, volatility trading can be a profitable strategy for options traders who are willing to take on some risk. By using options straddles and strangles, options spreads, or VIX ETFs, traders can take advantage of market volatility and potentially profit from price fluctuations. However, it is important to have a well-defined trading plan and to stay up-to-date on market news and trends to minimise risks and maximise profits.

The VIX (Volatility Index)

In the world of finance, volatility is one of the most important concepts to understand. It refers to the degree of variation in the price of a financial instrument over time. For traders, understanding volatility is crucial because it can affect the profitability of their investments. The VIX

(Volatility Index) is a measure of the expected volatility in the stock market over the next 30 days. In this topic, we will explore what the VIX is, how it works, and why it matters to options traders.

What is the VIX?

The VIX is often referred to as the "fear index" because it measures the level of fear or uncertainty in the stock market. It was created by the Chicago Board Options Exchange (CBOE) in 1993 as a way to gauge the market's expectation of future volatility. The VIX is calculated using the prices of S&P 500 index options and India VIX is a volatility index based on the NIFTY Index Option prices which reflects the market's consensus about the level of volatility in the near future.

How does the VIX work?

The VIX is based on the prices of options contracts, which give the holder the right to buy or sell a particular stock or index at a specific price. Options contracts are used by traders to speculate on the future direction of the market or to hedge against potential losses. The VIX is calculated using the prices of options contracts with different strike prices and expiration dates. These options contracts are used to create a synthetic option that mimics the behaviour of the S&P 500 index. The VIX is then derived from the price of this synthetic option.

Why does the VIX matter to options traders?

Options traders use the VIX as a tool to make informed decisions about their investments. When the VIX is high, it indicates that the market is expecting a high level of volatility in the near future. This can be a signal to options traders that it may be a good time to buy options contracts to hedge against potential losses or to speculate on the future direction of the market. Conversely, when the VIX is low, it indicates that the market is expecting a low level of volatility in the near future. This can be a signal to options traders that it may be a good time to sell options contracts or to take a more aggressive position in the market.

Understanding Implied and Historical Volatility

Volatility refers to the rate at which the price of an underlying asset moves up or down. In options trading, there are two types of volatility that traders need to understand: implied volatility and historical volatility.

Implied volatility is a measure of the market's expectation of how volatile an underlying asset will be in the future. It is calculated by using options prices and is expressed as a percentage. Implied volatility is an important factor in options pricing, as it influences the premium that traders pay when they buy an option. Generally, when the implied volatility of an underlying asset is high, the options premiums will also be high. Conversely, when implied volatility is low, options premiums will be relatively low.

Historical volatility, on the other hand, is a measure of how much an underlying asset has moved up or down in the past. It is calculated using the asset's historical price data and is also expressed as a percentage. Historical volatility is used to help options traders make informed decisions about the likelihood of an underlying asset moving up or down. For example, if the historical volatility of an asset has been low for a period of time, it may indicate that the asset is relatively stable and that options traders may want to consider selling options.

Options traders need to understand both implied and historical volatility in order to make informed decisions. Implied volatility is forward-looking and is based on expectations for the future. Historical volatility, on the other hand, is backward-looking and is based on past price movements. Both types of volatility can be used to help traders determine the potential risks and rewards of an options trade.

One common strategy that options traders use is to compare implied and historical volatility. If implied volatility is significantly higher than historical volatility, it may indicate that the market is expecting a significant price move in the future. This could be due to upcoming events such as earnings reports or political developments. In this scenario, options traders may want to consider buying options in order to take advantage of potential price movements.

Conversely, if implied volatility is significantly lower than historical volatility, it may indicate that the market is not expecting significant price movements in the future. In this scenario, options traders may want to consider selling options in order to generate income.

Options traders can also use volatility to assess the potential risks of an options trade. If the implied volatility of an asset is high, it may indicate that the market considers the asset to be risky. In this scenario, options traders may want to consider using strategies such as buying protective puts or selling covered calls in order to limit their potential losses.

In conclusion, options traders need to understand both implied and historical volatility in order to make informed decisions. Implied volatility is forward-looking and is based on expectations for the future, while historical volatility is backward-looking and is based on past price movements. Understanding these two types of volatility can help options traders assess potential risks and rewards, and determine the best strategies for their trades.

Strategies for Low and High Volatility Markets

It is important to have a strategy in place for both low and high volatility markets. These markets can be unpredictable and can cause significant losses if not approached with a solid plan. In this topic, we'll discuss some strategies that can be used in both low and high volatility markets.

Firstly, it's important to understand the difference between low and high volatility markets. A low volatility market is one where the price of the asset being traded is relatively stable and doesn't fluctuate too much. On the other hand, a high volatility market is one where the price of the asset being traded fluctuates significantly and is unpredictable.

In a low volatility market, one strategy that can be used is the iron condor. This strategy involves selling both a call and a put option at different strike prices. The goal is for the underlying asset to stay within a specific range of prices. If the asset stays within this range, both options will expire worthless, and the investor will keep the premium received from selling the options. If the asset moves outside of the range, the investor will incur a loss. However, the potential loss is limited to the difference between the strike prices of the options.

Another strategy that can be used in a low volatility market is the butterfly spread. This strategy involves buying a call option at a specific strike price while simultaneously selling two call options at higher and lower strike prices. The goal is for the underlying asset to stay close to the strike price of the purchased call option. If the asset stays within this range, the investor will profit from the premium received from selling the two call options. If the asset moves outside of the range, the investor will incur a loss. However, the potential loss is limited to the premium paid for the purchased call option.

In a high volatility market, one strategy that can be used is the straddle. This strategy involves buying both a call and a put option at the same strike price. The goal is for the underlying asset to move significantly in either direction. If the asset moves up, the call option will be profitable, and if the asset moves down, the put option will be profitable. The potential profit from this strategy is unlimited, but the potential loss is limited to the premium paid for both options.

Another strategy that can be used in a high volatility market is the strangle. This strategy involves buying both a call and a put option at different strike prices. The goal is for the underlying asset to move significantly in either direction, but not enough to reach the strike price of either option. If the asset moves in this way, both options will expire worthless, and the investor will keep the premium received from selling the options. If the asset moves outside of this range, the investor will incur a loss. However, the potential loss is limited to the difference between the strike prices of the options.

In conclusion, having a strategy in place for both low and high volatility markets is essential for any investor. Strategies such as the iron condor and butterfly spread can be used in low volatility markets, while the straddle and strangle can be used in high volatility markets. It's important to remember that these strategies come with risks, and investors should always do their own research and seek professional advice before investing.

CHAPTER 6

Trading Psychology and Discipline

T he stock market can be unpredictable. It requires a lot of discipline and a strong trading psychology to be able to navigate its ups and downs. In this chapter, we will discuss the importance of trading psychology and discipline in options trading.

Firstly, let's define what trading psychology is. Trading psychology refers to the emotional and mental state of a trader when making trading decisions. It includes emotions such as fear, greed, and hope. These emotions can cloud a trader's judgement and lead to poor trading decisions. Therefore, it is crucial for traders to have a strong trading psychology and be able to manage their emotions effectively.

One of the most important aspects of trading psychology is maintaining a positive attitude. As a trader, you will experience both wins and losses. It is important to stay positive and not let losses affect your trading decisions. If you let your emotions take over, you may make irrational decisions and compound your losses. Instead, focus on the long-term and stick to your trading plan.

Another important aspect of trading psychology is managing risk. As an options trader, you are already aware of the risks involved. It is important to have a solid risk management plan in place to protect your capital. This includes setting stop-loss orders and not risking more than you can afford to lose. By managing your risk effectively, you can avoid emotional trading decisions and protect your trading capital.

Discipline is also crucial in options trading. It is easy to get caught up in the excitement of the stock market and make impulsive trading decisions. However, this can lead to costly mistakes. It is important to have a trading plan and stick to it. This means setting clear entry and exit points and not deviating from them. By having a disciplined approach to trading, you can avoid making emotional decisions and improve your chances of success.

In addition, it is important to have a solid understanding of the options market and the underlying assets. This includes understanding the Greeks, such as delta and gamma, and how they impact your trades. It also includes conducting thorough research and analysis before making trading decisions. By having a deep understanding of the market, you can make informed decisions and avoid costly mistakes.

In conclusion, trading psychology and discipline are crucial for success in options trading. As a trader, it is important to have a strong trading psychology and be able to manage your emotions effectively. It is also important to have a disciplined approach to trading and stick to your trading plan. By managing risk, maintaining a positive attitude, and having a solid understanding of the market, you can improve your chances of success in options trading. Remember, the stock market can be unpredictable, but a disciplined and focused approach can help you navigate its ups and downs.

Common Psychological Pitfalls in Trading

Your success in the market depends on more than just your knowledge of the industry. It also depends on your ability to manage your emotions and avoid common psychological pitfalls that can sabotage your trades. In this topic, we'll explore some of the most common psychological pitfalls in trading, and provide tips for how to avoid them.

1. Fear and Greed

Fear and greed are two of the most powerful emotions that can affect your trading decisions. Fear can cause you to pull out of a trade too soon, while greed can cause you to hold onto a trade for too long. Both emotions can result in missed opportunities and lost profits.

To avoid falling victim to fear and greed, it's important to have a trading plan in place and stick to it. This means setting clear entry and exit points for each trade, and not deviating from those points based on emotions alone.

2. Confirmation Bias

Confirmation bias is the tendency to seek out information that confirms our existing beliefs, while ignoring information that contradicts them. In trading, this can lead to a dangerous cycle of self-fulfilling prophecies, where traders only see what they want to see and ignore warning signs that could lead to losses.

To avoid confirmation bias, it's important to remain open-minded and constantly reassess your strategies based on new information. This means seeking out diverse sources of information and considering multiple perspectives before making a trade.

3. Overconfidence

Overconfidence is the belief that you are better at trading than you actually are. This can lead to taking on too much risk, making impulsive trades, and failing to properly manage your portfolio.

To avoid overconfidence, it's important to be honest with yourself about your strengths and weaknesses as a trader. This means acknowledging when you've made a mistake and being willing to learn from it. It also means setting realistic goals and not taking on more risk than you can handle.

4. Loss Aversion

Loss aversion is the tendency to feel the pain of losses more acutely than the pleasure of gains. This can lead to holding onto losing positions for too long, in the hopes that they'll eventually turn around.

To avoid loss aversion, it's important to accept that losses are a natural part of trading and not to let them cloud your judgment. This means setting clear stop-loss points for each trade and sticking to them, even if it means taking a small loss.

5. Impulsivity

Impulsivity is the tendency to act on emotions rather than logic. In trading, this can lead to making trades based on gut feelings rather than careful analysis.

To avoid impulsivity, it's important to take a step back and assess each trade objectively. This means considering the potential risks and rewards of each trade, and not making a decision until you've carefully weighed all the factors.

In conclusion, it's important to be aware of the common psychological pitfalls that can affect your trading decisions. By staying disciplined, open-minded, and objective, you can avoid these pitfalls and increase your chances of success in the market.

Developing a Trading Plan

Creating a successful trading plan is an essential step for any options trader who wants to achieve long-term success in the market. By developing a well-crafted plan, traders can establish a clear path towards their financial goals, while also minimising risk and maximising profits.

The first step in developing a trading plan is to define your objectives. This could include specific financial targets, such as achieving a certain amount of profit within a specific timeframe, or more general goals, such as building a diverse investment portfolio. Whatever your objectives are, it is important to establish them early on, as they will provide a clear direction for your trading activities.

Once you have defined your objectives, the next step is to determine your risk tolerance. This involves assessing the level of risk you are willing to take on in pursuit of your financial goals. It is important to be realistic about your risk tolerance, as taking on too much risk can lead to significant losses, while being too cautious can limit your potential earnings.

After assessing your risk tolerance, you should then develop a trading strategy that aligns with your objectives and risk tolerance. This strategy should include details on the types of options you will trade, the markets you will focus on, and the specific indicators you will use to make trading decisions. It is important to test your strategy thoroughly in a demo account before implementing it with real money.

Another crucial element of a successful trading plan is risk management. This involves taking steps to limit your potential losses, such as using stop-loss orders or hedging strategies. It is also important to set realistic expectations for your returns, as aiming for unrealistic profits can lead to taking on excessive risk.

In addition to these elements, a trading plan should also include guidelines for record-keeping and analysis. By keeping detailed records of your trades, you can identify patterns and trends that can inform future trading decisions. Regularly analysing your performance can also help you identify areas for improvement and adjust your strategy accordingly.

Finally, it is important to regularly review and update your trading plan as needed. As markets change and your objectives evolve, your trading plan should adapt to reflect these changes. By regularly reviewing and revising your plan, you can ensure that it remains relevant and effective over the long term.

In conclusion, developing a trading plan is an essential step for any options trader who wants to achieve long-term success in the market. By defining your objectives, assessing your risk tolerance, developing a trading strategy, implementing risk management techniques, keeping detailed records, and regularly reviewing and updating your plan, you can establish a clear path towards your financial goals while minimising risk and maximising profits.

Emotional Control and Discipline

Emotional Control and Discipline are key traits that every options trader must possess. The ability to keep your emotions in check and stick to your trading plan is what separates successful traders from those who fail.

Firstly, it is important to understand that trading options is a game of probabilities. No matter how good you are, you will have losing trades. It is crucial to accept this fact and not let losses affect your emotions. It's easy to get carried away by greed and fear, but these emotions can cloud your judgment and lead to costly mistakes.

To maintain emotional control, it's important to have a well-defined trading plan. This should include your entry and exit points, stop-loss levels, and profit targets. Once you have a plan in place, stick to it. Do not deviate from it based on emotions or market noise. This will help you avoid impulsive decisions that could result in losses.

In addition to having a trading plan, it's important to have the discipline to follow it. This means having the patience to wait for the right opportunities and the discipline to cut your losses when necessary. Many traders fall into the trap of holding onto losing trades, hoping that the market will turn in their favour. This can result in significant losses and damage to your trading account.

To avoid this, it's important to set stop-loss levels for every trade. This will help you limit your losses and prevent them from spiralling out of control. It's also important to have the discipline to stick to these stop-loss levels, even if it means taking a small loss. Remember, a small loss is better than a large one.

Another important aspect of emotional control and discipline is risk management. Every trade you make should have a predefined risk/reward ratio. This means that you should never risk more than a certain percentage of your trading account on any single trade. This will help you manage your risk and avoid catastrophic losses.

In conclusion, emotional control and discipline are essential traits for every options trader. By having a well-defined trading plan, the discipline to follow it, and the ability to manage your risk, you can avoid emotional trading decisions and increase your chances of success. Remember, trading options is a game of probabilities, and losses are inevitable. The key is to keep your emotions in check and stick to your plan.

CHAPTER 7

Risk Mitigation and Hedging

T he world of options trading can be both exciting and nerve-wracking. On one hand, the potential for high returns is undeniable. On the other hand, the potential for significant losses is also a reality. That's why it's crucial for options traders to understand the concept of risk mitigation and hedging.

At its core, hedging is a strategy that traders use to limit the impact of potential losses. Essentially, it involves taking on a position that will offset the risk associated with another position. For example, imagine that you're an options trader who has a bullish outlook on a particular stock. You might decide to buy a call option, which would give you the right to buy the stock at a predetermined price. But what if the stock price doesn't rise as you had anticipated? You could end up losing a significant amount of money.

This is where hedging comes in. One way to hedge your call option position would be to purchase a put option at the same strike price. A put option gives you the right to sell the stock at a predetermined price. By holding both a call and a put option at the same strike price, you've effectively created a "collar" around the stock price. If the stock price rises, you'll make money on your call option, but if it falls, you'll make money on your put option. This way, you've limited your potential losses while still having the potential for gains.

Of course, hedging isn't foolproof, and it does come with its own set of risks. For one, it can be expensive to buy both a call and a put option. Additionally, if the stock price doesn't move much at all, you could end up losing money on both positions.

That's why it's important to understand that hedging is just one tool in the options trader's toolbox. It's not a one-size-fits-all solution, and it won't work in every situation. But when used judiciously, it can help to mitigate risk and limit losses.

Another way to mitigate risk in options trading is through diversification. By spreading your investments across multiple stocks or sectors, you can reduce the impact of any one stock's performance on your overall portfolio. For example, imagine that you're an options trader who has invested heavily in the technology sector. If a major tech company were to experience a significant downturn, your entire portfolio could be at risk. But if you had diversified your investments across multiple sectors, you'd be better protected against any one sector's performance.

Ultimately, the key to successful options trading is to have a solid understanding of the risks involved and to be prepared to mitigate those risks through strategies like hedging and diversification. While there's no surefire way to eliminate risk entirely, these tools can help to limit the impact of potential losses and allow traders to focus on the potential for gains. By staying informed, staying disciplined, and staying focused on the long-term, options traders can increase their chances of success in this exciting and dynamic market.

Hedging with Options

It's essential to have a solid understanding of hedging. Hedging is a risk-management strategy that helps protect your portfolio against market fluctuations. Options are an excellent tool for hedging, and in this topic, we'll explore the basics of hedging with options and provide a real-world example.

First, let's review the basics of options. Options give the buyer the right, but not the obligation, to buy or sell an underlying asset at a predetermined price (strike price) on or before a specific date (expiration date). There are two types of options: call options and put options. Call options give the buyer the right to buy the underlying asset, while put options give the buyer the right to sell the underlying asset.

Now, let's look at how options can be used for hedging. Suppose you hold a portfolio of stocks and are concerned about a potential market downturn. You could purchase put options on the stocks in your portfolio. If the market does indeed decline, the put options will increase in value, offsetting the losses in your stock holdings. This is known as a protective put strategy.

Let's say you own 100 shares of XYZ stock, currently trading at $50 per share. You're concerned about a potential market downturn and decide to purchase one XYZ put option with a strike price of $45 and an expiration date of three months from now. The cost of the put option is $2 per share or $200 total. If the market does decline, and XYZ stock drops to $40 per share in three months, the put option will be worth $5 per share, or $500 total. This offsets the loss in your stock holdings and results in a net gain of $300 ($500 from the put option minus the $200 cost of the option).

Another way options can be used for hedging is through a covered call strategy. This involves selling call options on stocks you already own. If the stock price remains below the strike price of the call option, the option will expire worthless, and you'll keep the premium (the amount you received for selling the option). This can help offset potential losses in your stock holdings.

For example, let's say you own 100 shares of ABC stock, currently trading at $75 per share. You decide to sell one ABC call option with a strike price of $80 and an expiration date of one month from now. The premium for the call option is $2 per share, or $200 total. If the stock price remains below $80, the call option will expire worthless, and you'll keep the $200 premium. If the stock price rises above $80, you'll be obligated to sell your shares at the strike price of $80, but you'll still keep the $200 premium. This helps offset any potential losses in your stock holdings if the stock price declines.

In summary, hedging with options can be an effective way to manage risk in your portfolio. Whether it's through a protective put or covered call strategy, options can help offset potential losses in your stock holdings and provide peace of mind during market downturns. As with any investment strategy, it's important to do your research and consult with a financial advisor before making any trades.

Reducing Portfolio Risk

As an options trader, it's important to be aware of the potential risks and take steps to mitigate them. In this topic, we'll discuss some strategies for reducing portfolio risk and protecting your investments.

- Diversify your portfolio
One of the most effective ways to reduce portfolio risk is to diversify your investments. This means spreading your money across different asset classes, industries, and companies. By doing so, you'll be less exposed to any one particular stock or sector, which will help protect your portfolio from volatility.

For options traders, diversification can also mean investing in different types of options contracts, such as calls and puts, as well as varying expiration dates and strike prices. This can help you hedge against potential losses and limit your exposure to any one particular trade.

- Set stop-loss orders

Another strategy for reducing portfolio risk is to set stop-loss orders. A stop-loss order is an instruction to sell a stock or option once it reaches a certain price. This can help you limit your losses in case a trade doesn't go as planned.

For options traders, stop-loss orders can be particularly useful because options can be highly volatile. By setting a stop-loss order, you can protect your investment and limit your losses if the underlying stock or index moves against you.

- Manage your position size

Position sizing is another important aspect of risk management for options traders. This means determining how much of your portfolio to allocate to each trade. By managing your position size, you can limit your exposure to any one particular trade and reduce your overall risk.

As a general rule, it's recommended that options traders allocate no more than 5% of their portfolio to any one trade. This can help you avoid overexposure to any one particular stock or option and protect your portfolio from volatility.

- Monitor the market

Finally, it's important to stay up-to-date on market trends and news. By monitoring the market, you'll be better equipped to make informed decisions about your investments and adjust your portfolio as needed.

For options traders, this means keeping an eye on the underlying stock or index, as well as any news or events that could impact the price of the option. By staying informed, you can make more strategic trades and reduce your overall risk.

In conclusion, reducing portfolio risk is an essential part of options trading. By diversifying your portfolio, setting stop-loss orders, managing your position size, and monitoring the market, you can protect your investments and reduce your exposure to volatility. Remember, investing always involves risk, but by taking these steps, you can help minimize that risk and increase your chances of success.

Portfolio Diversification

Diversification is the act of spreading your investments across different assets to minimize risk and maximize returns. In options trading, diversification can help you achieve a balanced portfolio that can withstand market volatility and provide steady profits.

One of the main benefits of diversification is that it can reduce risk. By investing in a variety of assets, you can reduce the impact of any single investment on your overall portfolio. This means that if one asset performs poorly, it will not have a significant impact on your entire portfolio. You can also benefit from the upside of different investments, which can help you achieve better long-term returns.

Another benefit of diversification is that it can help you manage your emotions. As an options trader, it's easy to get caught up in the excitement of a particular trade. However, if you have a diversified portfolio, you can avoid making impulsive decisions and stay focused on your overall investment strategy. This can help you avoid costly mistakes and keep your emotions in check.

Diversification can also help you achieve a more stable and consistent return on your investment. By investing in a variety of assets, you can spread your risk and reduce the impact of market fluctuations. This means that even if one asset is underperforming, you can still benefit from other investments that are performing well. This can help you achieve a more stable and predictable return on your investment over time.

So, how can you achieve a diversified options portfolio? One approach is to invest in different underlying assets, such as stocks, bonds, and commodities. It's important to note that diversification doesn't mean investing in random assets without a clear investment strategy. Instead, you should have a clear investment plan that aligns with your financial goals, risk tolerance, and investment horizon. You should also regularly review and rebalance your portfolio to ensure that it remains diversified and aligned with your investment strategy.

In summary, portfolio diversification is a key to successful options trading. By spreading your investments across different assets, you can minimize risk, manage your emotions, and achieve a stable and consistent return on your investment. To achieve a diversified options portfolio, you should invest in a mix of different options strategies and underlying assets, and have a clear investment plan that aligns with your financial goals.

CHAPTER 8

Advanced Trading Tools and Resources

The key to success in this field lies in having access to the right tools and resources. Luckily, the world of trading has evolved tremendously in recent years, and today there are more advanced trading tools and resources available than ever before. In this chapter, we will explore some of the most popular options trading tools and resources that can help you take your trading game to the next level.

One of the most powerful tools available to options traders today is the options trading platform. These platforms allow traders to access real-time market data, analyze trading patterns, and execute trades on the fly. Some of the most popular options trading platforms include Thinkorswim, E-Trade, and Interactive Brokers. These platforms offer a wide variety of features and tools that can help traders make informed decisions about their trades, including charting tools, options chains, and risk management tools.

Another essential resource for options traders is a quality options trading education. While it is possible to learn the basics of options trading on your own, a comprehensive education program can help you build a solid foundation of knowledge and skills that will serve you well in your trading career. There are many options for trading education programs available, ranging from online courses to in-person seminars. Some of the most reputable options trading education providers include the Options Industry Council, Investopedia, and the Chicago Board Options Exchange.

If you are looking for a more hands-on approach to options trading education, you may want to consider joining an options trading community. These communities are made up of like-minded traders who share their knowledge, experience, and insights with one another. Many options trading communities offer educational resources, such as webinars, forums, and chat rooms, as well as opportunities to collaborate on trades and strategies. Some of the most popular options trading communities include the Options Trading Reddit community, the Options Trading Club, and the Options Trading Pro System.

In addition to trading platforms and education resources, there are many other tools and resources that options traders can use to improve their trading results. One such tool is the options scanner, which allows traders to scan the market for potential trading opportunities based on specific criteria, such as price, volume, and volatility. Some of the most popular options scanners include Trade-Ideas, Options Hawk, and Livevol.

Risk management is another key aspect of successful options trading, and there are many resources available to help traders manage their risk effectively. One such resource is the options calculator, which allows traders to calculate the theoretical value of their options and assess the potential risks and rewards of a trade. There are many options calculators available online, including the CBOE Options Calculator and the Options Profit Calculator.

In conclusion, if you are an options trader looking to improve your trading results, there are many advanced trading tools and resources available to help you achieve your goals. Whether you are looking for a powerful trading platform, a comprehensive education program, or a community of like-minded traders, there is something out there for everyone. By taking advantage of these resources, you can gain the knowledge, skills, and confidence you need to become a successful options trader.

Trading Platforms and Software

As a trader, one of the most important tools at your disposal is a reliable and efficient trading platform. Trading platforms and software are essential for executing trades, analyzing market data, and managing your portfolio. With so many different options available, it can be difficult to know where to turn. In this topic, we'll take a closer look at trading platforms and software and help you determine which one is right for you.

When it comes to trading platforms, there are two main options: web-based platforms and downloadable software. Web-based platforms are accessible through your internet browser and usually require no downloads or installations. They are convenient and can be accessed from any device with an internet connection. Downloadable software, on the other hand, is installed directly onto your computer. While this option may require more setup time, it typically offers more advanced features and a more customizable experience.

When selecting a trading platform, it's important to consider your individual needs and preferences. Some traders prefer a sleek and simple interface, while others require more advanced charting and analytical tools. Additionally, if you plan on trading on the go, mobile compatibility may be a key factor for you. Many trading platforms offer mobile apps that allow you to trade from your smartphone or tablet.

Another important consideration is the level of support and resources offered by the platform. Look for a platform that offers educational materials, customer support, and a community of traders to connect with. This can be especially helpful for beginners who are just starting out in the world of options trading.

One popular trading platform is thinkorswim, offered by TD Ameritrade. Thinkorswim is a downloadable software that offers advanced charting and analytical tools, as well as a customizable interface. It also offers a variety of educational resources, including webinars and tutorials, to help traders of all levels improve their skills.

Another option is the web-based platform offered by TradingView. TradingView offers a simple and intuitive interface, as well as a mobile app for on-the-go trading. It also offers a wide range of educational materials, including articles, videos, and webinars.

Regardless of which platform you choose, it's important to remember that no platform is perfect. Each has its own strengths and weaknesses, and what works for one trader may not work for another. It's important to do your research, read reviews, and take advantage of any demo or trial periods offered by the platform to ensure that it meets your individual needs and preferences.

In conclusion, trading platforms and software are an essential tool for options traders. When selecting a platform, it's important to consider your individual needs and preferences, as well as the level of support and resources offered by the platform. There are many different options available, each with its own strengths and weaknesses. By doing your research and taking advantage of demo or trial periods, you can find the platform that is right for you and take your options trading to the next level.

Option Chains and Greeks

Understanding option chains and Greeks is crucial to your success in the market. Option chains and Greeks are two essential tools that can help you make informed decisions about your options trades. In this complete guide, we will cover everything you need to know about option chains and Greeks, including how they work, what they are used for, and how to use them to your advantage.

Option Chains

Option chains are a listing of all available options for a particular stock or index. They contain information on the strike price, expiration date, and premium price for each option. Option chains are typically organized by expiration date, with the closest expiration dates listed first.

One of the primary uses of option chains is to help traders identify potential trades. Traders can use option chains to compare the prices of different options and determine which ones are the most attractive. For example, if a trader believes that a stock is going to increase in price, they may look for call options with a strike price that is slightly above the current stock price. By comparing the premiums for different call options with the same expiration date, the trader can identify the option with the lowest premium and the highest potential profit.

Option chains are also useful for managing open trades. Traders can use them to monitor the prices of their open positions and determine when to close them out. For example, if a trader has a call option that is in the money and the expiration date is approaching, they may use the option chain to determine the best time to sell the option and lock in their profits.

Greeks

Greeks are a set of mathematical calculations that are used to measure the risk and potential profitability of options trades. There are five main Greeks that traders use: delta, gamma, theta, vega, and rho.

Delta is a measure of how much an option's price will change in relation to the underlying asset's price. It ranges from 0 to 1 for call options (0 to -1 for put options) and is affected by factors such as the strike price, expiration date, and volatility of the underlying asset.

Gamma is a measure of how much an option's delta will change in relation to the underlying asset's price. It ranges from 0 to 1 and is affected by factors such as the time remaining until expiration and the volatility of the underlying asset.

Theta is a measure of how much an option's price will change as time passes. It is affected by factors such as the time remaining until expiration, the strike price, and the volatility of the underlying asset.

Vega is a measure of how much an option's price will change in relation to changes in volatility. It is affected by factors such as the time remaining until expiration, the strike price, and the underlying asset's historical volatility.

Rho is a measure of how much an option's price will change in relation to changes in interest rates. It is affected by factors such as the time remaining until expiration, the strike price, and the underlying asset's interest rate.

Using Option Chains and Greeks

To use option chains and Greeks effectively, traders need to have a good understanding of how they work and how to interpret the information they provide. Traders should also be familiar with different trading strategies and how to apply them to different market conditions.

One common strategy that traders use is the covered call strategy. This involves selling call options on a stock that you own in order to generate additional income. Traders can use the option chain to identify the best strike price and expiration date for their call options, while also using the Greeks to manage their risk and potential profitability.

- Conclusion

Option chains and Greeks are powerful tools that can help traders make informed decisions about their options trades. By using option chains to identify potential trades and manage open positions, and using Greeks to measure risk and potential profitability, traders can increase their chances of success in the market. By mastering these tools and applying them to different trading strategies, traders can take their options trading to the next level.

Staying Updated with Market Trends

Markets are dynamic, and trends can change in no time. Therefore, it's essential to keep yourself informed about the market happenings to make informed decisions. In this topic, we will discuss some tips on how to stay updated with market trends.

1. Follow Market News

The first and most crucial step in staying updated with market trends is to follow market news. The news provides an insight into what's happening in the market and what's likely to happen in the future. You should follow reputable news sources that cover market trends, such as Bloomberg, Wall Street Journal, and Reuters. You can subscribe to their newsletters or follow them on social media to stay updated.

2. Attend Conferences and Seminars

Attending conferences and seminars is a great way to stay updated with market trends. These events bring together industry experts, traders, and investors to discuss market trends and share their insights. You can learn a lot from attending these events, and you can also network with other traders and investors.

3. Join Trading Communities

Joining trading communities is another excellent way to stay updated with market trends. These communities bring together traders and investors from different parts of the world. You can learn from their experiences and share your own. You can also get access to market insights and analysis that you may not find elsewhere.

4. Use Trading Platforms

Trading platforms can also help you stay updated with market trends. These platforms provide a wealth of information, such as real-time quotes, news, and analysis. You can also use these platforms to monitor your trades and make informed decisions.

5. Read Trading Blogs

Reading trading blogs is another great way to stay updated with market trends. There are many trading blogs out there that cover market trends, trading strategies, and other related topics. You can subscribe to these blogs or follow them on social media to stay updated.

6. Analyze Market Data

Analyzing market data is also crucial in staying updated with market trends. You should study market data and analyze it to identify trends and patterns. You can use various tools and software to analyze market data, such as TradingView, Finviz, and Thinkorswim.

In conclusion, staying updated with market trends is crucial for your success as an options trader. You should follow market news, attend conferences and seminars, join trading communities, use trading platforms, read trading blogs, and analyze market data. By doing so, you can make informed decisions and stay ahead of the curve.

Remember, the market is dynamic, and staying updated is an ongoing process.

CHAPTER 9

Advanced Order Types and Execution

raders are always looking for ways to maximize their profits while minimising the risks. One way to do this is by using advanced order types and execution strategies. In this chapter, we will explore some of these options and how they can benefit you as a trader.

First, let's talk about order types. The most basic order type is a market order, which is executed at the current market price. This is great if you need to get in or out of a trade quickly, but it doesn't give you any control over the price you pay or receive. This is where limit orders come in. A limit order allows you to set a specific price at which you want to buy or sell an option. This gives you more control over your trades, but it also means that your order might not get filled if the price doesn't reach your limit.

Another type of order is a stop order, which is triggered when the market reaches a certain price. A stop order can be used to limit your losses or to lock in profits. For example, if you are long a call option and the price starts to drop, you could place a stop order to sell the option if the price falls below a certain level. This would limit your losses if the price continues to drop. On the other hand, if the price is rising, you could place a stop order to sell the option if the price falls below a certain level. This would lock in your profits if the price starts to reverse.

Market Orders vs. Limit Orders

Both types of orders can be used to buy or sell options, but they work in different ways and have different advantages and disadvantages.

Market orders are the most common type of order used by traders. When you place a market order, you're telling your broker to buy or sell an option at the current market price. This means that your order will be executed immediately, but the price you get may not be exactly what you expected. This is because the price of an option can change quickly, and there may not be enough buyers or sellers at the exact price you want.

For example, let's say you want to buy a call option on XYZ stock. The current market price is $50 per share, and you're willing to pay up to $55 per share for the option. If you place a market order, your broker will buy the option for you at the best available price, which may be higher than $55 if there are no sellers at that price. On the other hand, if you want to sell an option at the current market price, a market order will ensure that your order is filled quickly, but you may not get the best possible price.

Limit orders, on the other hand, allow you to set a specific price at which you want to buy or sell an option. When you place a limit order, your broker will only execute your order if the option's price reaches your specified limit price. This means that you have more control over the price you get, but your order may not be filled immediately if the market price doesn't reach your limit.

For example, let's say you want to buy a call option on XYZ stock, and you're only willing to pay $55 per share. If you place a limit order, your broker will only buy the option if the price drops to $55 or lower. If the price never reaches $55, your order will not be executed. Similarly, if you want to sell an option at a specific price, a limit order can ensure that you get the price you want, but your order may not be filled if the market price doesn't reach your limit.

So which type of order should you use as an options trader? It depends on your trading strategy and goals. If you want to buy or sell an option quickly and don't care as much about the exact price, a market order may be the best choice. On the other hand, if you want more control over the price you get and are willing to wait for the right price, a limit order may be a better option.

It's also worth noting that different brokers may have different rules and fees for market and limit orders. Some brokers may charge higher fees for limit orders, for example, or may only allow certain types of orders for certain types of options. Be sure to check with your broker and understand their rules before placing any trades.

In summary, understanding the difference between market orders and limit orders is important. Market orders are executed immediately at the current market price, while limit orders allow you to specify a price at which you want to buy or sell an option. Both types of orders have their advantages and disadvantages, and the type you choose should depend on your trading strategy and goals.

Stop Orders and Stop-Limit Orders

A stop order is an instruction to buy or sell an asset once it reaches a certain price. This can be useful in a variety of scenarios, such as when you want to limit your losses or lock in profits.

For example, let's say you own a call option that's currently valued at $2.50 per contract. You could set a stop order to sell that option if its price drops to $2.00 per contract. This means that if the option's value starts to decline, you'll automatically sell it before it drops too low and erodes your profits.

Stop orders come in two flavors: market and limit. A market order means that you'll sell or buy the asset at the best available price once it hits your stop price. This can be useful if you want to get out of a position quickly, but it can also lead to slippage if the market is volatile.

On the other hand, a limit order means that you'll only sell or buy the asset at a specific price or better once it hits your stop price. This can be useful if you want to have more control over the execution price, but it can also mean that your order won't be executed if the price doesn't reach your limit.

Another type of order you might want to consider is the stop-limit order. This is a combination of a stop order and a limit order. With a stop-limit order, you set both a stop price and a limit price. If the asset hits your stop price, a limit order is triggered at your limit price.

For example, let's say you own a put option that's currently valued at $3.00 per contract. You could set a stop-limit order to sell that option if its price drops to $2.50 per contract, with a limit price of $2.00 per contract. This means that if the option's value starts to decline, you'll automatically sell it at or above $2.00 per contract.

Stop-limit orders can be useful in volatile markets where prices can change rapidly. They can help you avoid slippage and ensure that you get a fair price for your asset.

Overall, stop orders and stop-limit orders are powerful tools that options traders can use to manage risk and maximize profits. By setting these orders, you can ensure that you're staying on top of your investments and making informed decisions. Just remember to use them wisely and always have a plan in place for every trade you make.

Advanced Order Types (e.g., OCO, Trailing Stops)

There are a variety of order types available to help you manage your positions. But have you considered using advanced order types like One-Cancels-the-Other (OCO) or Trailing Stops?

OCO orders allow you to place two orders simultaneously, with the condition that if one is executed, the other is cancelled. For example, let's say you have a long call option on Company X, but you're worried about a potential market downturn. You could place an OCO order to simultaneously sell the call if the stock price drops below a certain level, or sell it if it rises above a certain level. This way, you can protect your profits or limit your losses without having to constantly monitor the position.

Trailing Stops are another advanced order type that can be useful for options traders. With a Trailing Stop, you set a percentage or dollar amount below the current market price for a long position, or above the current market price for a short position. If the price moves in your favour, the Trailing Stop will move with it. But if the price starts to move against you, the Trailing Stop will trigger a sell order at the specified price. This can help you lock in profits while also limiting potential losses.

Of course, there are some potential downsides to using advanced order types like OCO or Trailing Stops. For one thing, they can be more complex than traditional order types and may require a bit more research and experimentation to get right. Additionally, some brokers may charge extra fees for using advanced order types, so be sure to read the fine print before placing any trades.

That being said, if you're willing to put in the time and effort to learn how to use advanced order types effectively, they can be a powerful tool for managing your options positions. Just remember to always do your research and keep an eye on the market, as even the most sophisticated order types can't protect you from unexpected events or sudden market shifts.

In conclusion, advanced order types like OCO and Trailing Stops can be a valuable addition to any options trader's toolkit. By allowing you to set up automated trades that protect your profits and limit your losses, these order types can help you stay on top of your positions even when you're not actively monitoring the market. Just be sure to do your due diligence before using any advanced order types, and always keep an eye on the market to ensure that your trades are working as intended.

Tips for Efficient Order Execution

One of the most critical aspects of your job is to execute orders efficiently. It is the key to success in this field. Efficient order execution not only saves time but also helps you to make more profits. If you execute orders efficiently, you can maximize your earnings and minimize your losses. Here are some tips for efficient order execution that can help you become a successful options trader.

1. Use Limit Orders

Using limit orders is one of the most effective ways to execute orders efficiently. A limit order allows you to specify the maximum or minimum price at which you want to buy or sell an option. When the market reaches your desired price, the order is executed automatically. This way, you can avoid missing out on opportunities and prevent slippage.

2. Monitor the Market

To execute orders efficiently, you need to be aware of the market. You should monitor the market regularly to stay up-to-date with the latest news and trends. This will help you make informed decisions and execute orders at the right time. You can use various tools and resources to monitor the market, such as financial news websites, social media, and trading platforms.

3. Set Realistic Goals

Setting realistic goals is essential for efficient order execution. You should have a clear idea of what you want to achieve and set achievable targets. This will help you avoid making impulsive decisions and executing orders without proper analysis. You should also be realistic about your expectations and avoid taking unnecessary risks.

4. Use Stop-Loss Orders

Stop-loss orders are an effective way to minimize losses and protect your capital. A stop-loss order is an instruction to sell an option when it reaches a certain price. This way, you can limit your losses and prevent yourself from losing more than you can afford. Stop-loss orders can also help you avoid emotional trading and prevent impulsive decisions.

5. Keep a Trading Journal

Keeping a trading journal is an excellent way to improve your performance and execute orders efficiently. You should record all your trades, including the entry and exit prices, the size of the position, and the reason for the trade. This will help you analyze your performance, identify your strengths and weaknesses, and make improvements accordingly.

In conclusion, efficient order execution is crucial for success in options trading. You should use limit orders, monitor the market, set realistic goals, use stop-loss orders, and keep a trading journal to execute orders efficiently. These tips will help you make informed decisions, minimize losses, and maximize profits. Remember to stay disciplined, patient, and focused, and you will be on your way to becoming a successful options trader.

CHAPTER 10

The Road to The Perfect Trade

T he road to the perfect trade can feel like an endless journey. There are countless factors to consider, from market trends to individual stock performance. But fear not, with careful planning and a bit of patience, you can improve your chances of making successful trades.

The first step on the road to the perfect trade is to do your research. Before making any investment, it's important to thoroughly analyze the market and the specific stock you're considering buying or selling options for. Look at historical trends, current events, and anything else that could impact the stock's performance.

Next, consider the risk-reward ratio of the trade. While it's tempting to go after high-risk, high-reward trades, it's important to remember that these also come with a higher chance of failure. Instead, aim for trades with a balanced risk-reward ratio that aligns with your personal risk tolerance.

Another important factor to consider is timing. When entering a trade, make sure to have a clear exit strategy in place. This could be a specific price at which you will sell the option or a predetermined time frame in which you plan to exit the trade. By having a plan in place, you can avoid making impulsive decisions based on emotions rather than logic.

It's also important to keep an eye on the overall market trends. While individual stock performance is important, the broader market can also impact your trades. Look for patterns in the market and adjust your trades accordingly.

Finally, don't be afraid to seek out advice from experts in the field. Whether it's through online forums or consulting with a financial advisor, getting a second opinion can help you feel more confident in your trades.

In summary, the road to the perfect trade requires careful planning, research, and a bit of patience. By analyzing market trends, considering risk-reward ratios, timing your trades, keeping an eye on the broader market, and seeking out advice, you can increase your chances of becoming a successful trader. Remember, success in trading is a marathon, not a sprint. Stay focused and disciplined, and over time you'll see the fruits of your labour.

Setting Realistic Goals

It is important to set realistic goals in order to achieve success in your trading journey. Setting goals can help you stay focused and motivated, as well as provide a clear direction for your trading strategy. However, it is important to set goals that are achievable and realistic, rather than lofty and unattainable.

The first step in setting realistic goals is to assess your current trading performance. Take a look at your past trades and analyze your successes and failures. This will give you a better understanding of your strengths and weaknesses as a trader and will help you identify areas where you need to improve. Once you have a clear understanding of your trading performance, you can begin to set goals that are tailored to your unique situation.

When setting goals, it is important to be specific and measurable. Rather than setting a vague goal like "make more money," set a specific goal such as "earn a profit of $500 per week." This will give you a clear target to aim for, and will help you track your progress over time. It is also important to set a timeframe for achieving your goals. This will help you stay focused and motivated and will give you a sense of urgency to take action.

Another key factor in setting realistic goals is to consider your risk tolerance. Every trader has a different risk tolerance, and it is important to set goals that align with your comfort level. If you are a conservative trader, setting a goal to earn a profit of $10,000 per month may be unrealistic. Instead, focus on setting goals that are achievable based on your risk tolerance and trading style.

In addition to setting goals, it is important to have a plan in place for achieving them. This plan should include specific actions that you will take in order to reach your goals, as well as a timeline for completing these actions. For example, if your goal is to earn a profit of $500 per week, your plan may include actions such as analyzing market trends, identifying potential trades, and executing trades based on your analysis.

Finally, it is important to review your goals and progress on a regular basis. This will help you stay on track and identify areas where you may need to make adjustments. If you find that you are consistently falling short of your goals, it may be time to reevaluate your trading strategy and make changes as needed.

In conclusion, setting realistic goals is a critical component of a successful trader. By assessing your trading performance, setting specific and measurable goals, considering your risk tolerance, creating a plan of action, and regularly reviewing your progress, you can stay focused and motivated on your trading journey. Remember, success as a trader is a journey, not a destination, and setting realistic goals is key to achieving your long-term trading goals.

Epilogue: The Journey Continues

Closing Words. As you turn the final pages of "**The Perfect Trade** | Options Made Simple: A Beginner's Guide to Profitable Options Trading", you're not reaching an end; you're reaching a new beginning. Your journey into the world of options trading and technical analysis has been a transformative one, filled with insights, strategies, and the pursuit of mastery. Rome wasn't built in a day, and neither is trading mastery. Patience is essential. There will be setbacks, losses, and challenges along the way. But remember, every great trader faced adversity before reaching the pinnacle of success.

But this book is not the destination; it is a waypoint on your journey to trading excellence. The knowledge you've gained here, from understanding the intricacies of options to deciphering the language of charts, is just the foundation. It's what you do next that will define your path.

The financial markets are ever-evolving, and staying ahead requires continuous learning. Whether you're a seasoned trader or just beginning, commit to ongoing education. Explore advanced courses, attend seminars, and read widely. The more you learn, the sharper your trading edge becomes. The markets are dynamic, and what works today may not work tomorrow. Be adaptable. Be willing to innovate and explore new strategies. Flexibility is a trader's asset in an ever-changing landscape.

Trading can be a solitary pursuit, but it doesn't have to be. Engage with trading communities, both online and offline. Share experiences, insights, and strategies with fellow traders. Mentorship from experienced traders can provide invaluable guidance on your journey.

Every trader has a "why." It's the reason you started this journey, whether it's to secure your financial future, provide for your family, or achieve a lifelong dream. Your "why" is your motivation, your driving force. Keep it front and centre as a reminder of what's at stake and what you're working toward.

This epilogue is not the end; it's a reminder that your journey is ongoing. Your pursuit of trading mastery is a lifelong endeavor, filled with challenges, triumphs, and endless possibilities. With the knowledge and skills you've acquired, you are well-prepared to navigate the complexities of financial markets and continue your quest for the perfect trade.

So, step boldly into the future, embrace the opportunities that lie ahead, and let your journey to trading excellence be a testament to your determination and dedication.

Thank you for taking the time to read the book. The world of trading awaits you.

www.ingramcontent.com/pod-product-compliance
Lightning Source LLC
Chambersburg PA
CBHW022343290526
45786CB00014B/2383